D0894060

COUNTDOWN TO SPACE

SPACECHIMP
NASA's Ape in Space

Melinda Farbman and Frye Gaillard

Series Advisor:
John E. McLeaish
Chief, Public Information Office, retired,
NASA Johnson Space Center

Enslow Publishers, Inc.

40 Industrial Road   PO Box 38
Box 398   Aldershot
Berkeley Heights, NJ 07922 Hants GU12 6BP
USA   UK
http://www.enslow.com

Library of Congress Cataloging-in-Publication Data

Farbman, Melinda.
   Spacechimp : NASA's ape in space / Melinda Farbman and Frye Gaillard.
     p. cm. — (Countdown to space)
     Includes bibliographical references and index.
     Summary: Describes the life of the chimpanzee that was sent into space as
part of the American space program, describing his capture, training, the actual
flight, and his life afterward.
     ISBN 0-7660-1478-9
     1. Spaceflight Juvenile literature. 2. Ham (Chimpanzee) Juvenile literature.
3. Chimpanzees Biography Juvenile literature. 4. Chimpanzees as laboratory
animals Juvenile literature. [1. Ham (Chimpanzee) 2. Chimpanzees.
3. Spaceflight.] I. Gaillard, Frye, 1946–   . II. Title. III. Series.
TL793.F37   2000
629.45—dc21

                                         99-39206
                                            CIP

Printed in the United States of America

10 9 8 7 6 5 4 3 2 1

To Our Readers: All Internet addresses in this book were active and appropriate
when we went to press. Any comments or suggestions can be sent by e-mail to
Comments@enslow.com or to the address on the back cover.

Photo Credits: © Corel Corporation, p. 7; Edward C. Dittmer, Sr., and the
United States Air Force, pp. 10, 17, 19, 27, 35; National Aeronautics and
Space Administration (NASA), pp. 4, 8, 13, 15, 20, 23, 25, 29, 31, 33, 34, 41;
Photo Courtesy of the North Carolina Zoological Park, pp. 38, 41 (inset).

Cover Photo: NASA (foreground); Raghvendra Sahai and John Trauger
(JPL), the WFPC2 science team, NASA, and AURA/STScI (background).

CONTENTS

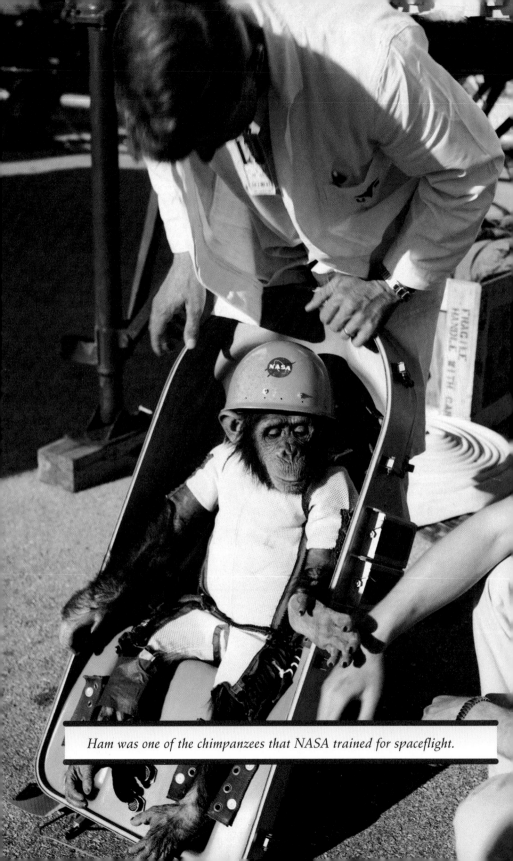

Ham was one of the chimpanzees that NASA trained for spaceflight.

1

The Early Pioneers

Deep in a jungle of Africa, in a place called the Cameroons, there lived a baby chimpanzee. He was like others of his kind. He ate bugs and fruit. He held onto the hair of his mother's back and rode her through the rain forest. As the baby chimp grew, he hung on branches, patted his toes, and pulled sticks from other chimps. He threw his arms around his mother and jumped on her belly. At night he slept high in a tree, but not as far from Earth as he soon would go.[1]

This baby chimpanzee would soar from a rocket into space. He would become the famous astrochimp named Ham, who led the way for American astronauts to go into space, around Earth, to the Moon, and beyond.[2]

One day, the baby chimpanzee was captured from

the jungle and taken to the United States.[3] There, scientists, engineers, and test pilots were busy finding ways to send a human into space. They wanted to explore space faster and better than any other country in the world, especially the Soviet Union.

In their race to understand space, Americans sent plants and animals into the sky. Fruit flies and fungus spores, mice and hamsters, and cats and dogs took rocket trips. Many Rhesus monkeys went into space, too. Mike and Pat reached an altitude, or height, of 36 miles.[4] Able and Baker went 300 miles high at the speed of 10,000 miles per hour, and landed safely in the ocean.[5] At the speed of 3,685 miles per hour, Sam reached a height of 51 miles. Just forty-five days after his flight, Miss Sam was launched. She went nine miles high and hugged Sam when she returned to Earth.[6]

These Rhesus monkeys took suborbital flights. The rockets had enough power to send the capsules away from Earth in the direction of a straight line. Once launched, the capsules traveled far, but as they spent energy soaring out against gravity, they lost speed. Eventually, the capsules slowed enough to give in to the pull of gravity and drop back to Earth. In the same way that a ball thrown up always comes down, a suborbital flight goes straight out and directly back to Earth again. For a while, suborbital missions were the only kind that Americans tried.

In the African jungle, chimpanzees play with members of their group. Young chimps were taken to the United States for use in NASA's space program.

But the Soviet Union was more ambitious. One day in 1960, the Soviets sent two dogs named Strelka and Belka even farther than the height of a suborbital flight. A rocket lifted the dogs' capsule with so much power that it did not fall back to Earth. Instead of falling into the ocean, their capsule fell around Earth. It was in orbit. Strelka and Belka orbited the earth eighteen times. They survived the trip, and later had puppies.[7]

This was a happier ending to an orbital flight than the one the Soviets had experienced in 1957. In November of that year, a stray dog named Laika orbited Earth for a week. She was in a satellite called *Sputnik 2*. Although this famous vehicle was the first to carry a

Astronaut Alan B. Shepard, Jr., the first American in space, inspects his spacecraft after returning from the first manned suborbital spaceflight, May 5, 1961. This accomplishment was made possible by the animals that flew into space first to test the safety of spaceflight.

living thing into orbit, its passenger, Laika, died after ten days.

For all the experiments that Americans and Soviets tried, space was still full of mysteries in the 1950s and 1960s. Many dangers awaited the first human space travelers. Would they survive the speed of a rocket? Would they mind floating inside their capsule when gravity began to lessen? What about the heat that would sear the capsule as it tore back through the gases that surround Earth? What about the final splashdown into the ocean?

The Americans who devoted themselves to finding answers to these questions called their work Project Mercury. Their goal was to send a person into space and back again alive—and they knew that accidents could happen. They decided to risk the life of a chimpanzee before risking the life of a human being.[8]

2

In the Lab

The first job of Project Mercury was to teach chimpanzees how to use instruments in space the way a human astronaut would. The United States Air Force helped by training the animals. They knew that if a chimp could think and act in space, a human probably could, because chimps and humans are in some ways similar. Chimpanzees are intelligent creatures, like humans. They have bodies with organs inside that are arranged the way humans' hearts, lungs, and stomachs are arranged. They also have thumbs for gripping things. Most important, chimps have a nervous system that is much like humans'. It lets chimps react to lights and sounds almost as quickly as people do. Quick reaction time is important in space travel. Astronauts must press buttons and flip levers calmly and quickly to steer a craft. As Project Mercury began, Air Force officers at Holloman Air Force Base in Alamogordo, New Mexico, gave flight lessons to twenty baby chimps. One of them was Ham.[1]

A man named Colonel Stapp made sure that the chimps were given good medical care and lots of affection. He dismissed anyone who mistreated an animal.[2] The Air Force veterinarians, Colonel Brunsky, Dr. Cook, Dr. Fineg, and others, cuddled the chimps. They checked the chimpanzees before every flight training session to make sure they were healthy. They gave the animals lemon drops after each checkup. To

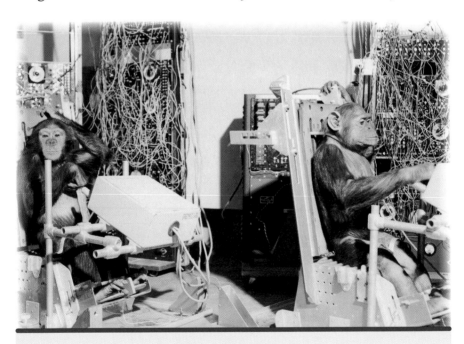

Because chimpanzees are so intelligent, they were able to learn to complete tasks, in preparation for a trip to space.

prevent infection, the vets gave the animals antibiotics in spoonfuls of raspberry gelatin.[3]

The humans and the chimps soon became close friends. As the men grew to know the animals' personalities, they gave them names. There were Billy, Minnie, Elvis, and Bobby Joe. Ham's official name during training was Chimp #65. His trainers liked to call him Chang. It was not until after his flight that Chang became known as Ham.[4]

Edward C. Dittmer, Sr., spent every day training Ham for his space trip. Dittmer was a pilot who often flew an F-94 plane to 30,000 feet and dropped it toward Earth. His plane fell back to Earth at the same rate that Earth pulled it. He was moving with gravity, not against it. He felt no weight. He floated. For forty-five seconds, he felt zero gravity. One day when he did this, the peanuts that he had with him for lunch floated above his nose.

Sometimes, Dittmer flew his plane against gravity. He barreled toward the sky at a speed that made him feel very heavy. Often he felt so heavy that he would black out. He and other pilots did this many times. They were curious about what would happen to people in space.

After a time, Dittmer knew a great deal about the human body and high altitudes. He also knew about medicine. He had cared for wounded soldiers in a hospital after World War II. As an Air Force officer who knew about space biology, Dittmer had much to share with Ham. He used everything he knew to train him.

Ham had a good temper. He let Dittmer hold him. Playfully, Ham wrapped his long hairy arms around the man as they worked together. Dittmer began training Ham by teaching him how to sit in a small metal chair. He was careful to place all the chimps in chairs four or five feet apart. That way they would not be able to reach out and play with each other, which they liked to do. Ham wore a small web jacket to keep him in the chair. Dittmer gave him fruit and toys to play with. At first, Ham stayed in the chair for only five minutes.[5] He did not want to stay still. But "Ham was a real gentleman," said Dittmer. "He was a good animal, laughing all the time."[6] Slowly, Ham gave in to his trainer. As time passed, the chimps learned to sit for most of the day.

After Ham had learned to use a chair, Dittmer taught him how to use an aluminum couch. The couch supported Ham's entire spine and head. It held him in place as he rode the special vehicles that had been made to simulate, or copy, space travel. Ham experienced zero gravity in the padded interior of a C131 airplane. Dittmer flew the plane straight up, then curved into an arc in the sky. While they flew in the arc, Ham and Dittmer floated inside the plane. Dittmer checked the instruments attached to Ham to see if they worked during this free fall.

In the lab, Ham learned what it would feel like to accelerate, or travel at greater and greater speeds. He was placed in a centrifuge, a machine that whirls around like

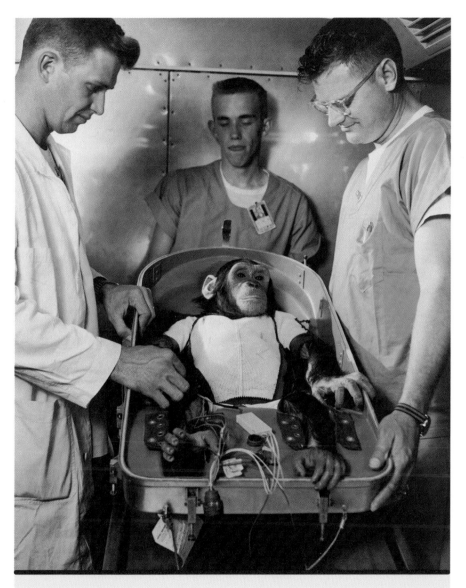

Edward Dittmer (right) looks on at one of the chimps specially trained for the MR-2 flight. The chimp is in the couch in which it will ride during the sixteen-minute flight from Cape Canaveral.

a top. In the same way that water stays in a swinging bucket, Ham was pulled up against the side of the swirling machine by centrifugal force. Dittmer observed Ham to see how he managed the extra weight of such force, for Ham would feel it on his way into space. At times, Ham had to sit all alone for hours in a small chamber. This helped him become familiar with the great loneliness of space.[7]

Suited up and strapped to his couch, Ham spent many hours pulling levers and pushing buttons, the way an astronaut would to steer his spacecraft. Ham would never learn to control the direction of his craft, but he learned other tasks.[8] Ham watched white and blue lights flash and learned what they meant. If he pulled certain levers quickly enough in response to the lights, he would not feel a mild electric shock. Dittmer had attached metal plates to the fleshy palms of Ham's feet. They were attached to electric wires. If Ham responded to the lights too slowly, he felt the electrical current in his body. It was a sensation he did not want to feel. Luckily, Ham was fast enough to avoid shocks. He had learned to pull the correct lever once every twenty seconds.

Sometimes Ham made judgments. Three shapes flashed before his eyes: two triangles and a circle.[9] Ham saw that the circle was different. Quickly, he hit the lever beneath that shape. For noticing which shape was different, he earned a prize. Banana-flavored pellets dropped into a cup beneath his busy hands. He also

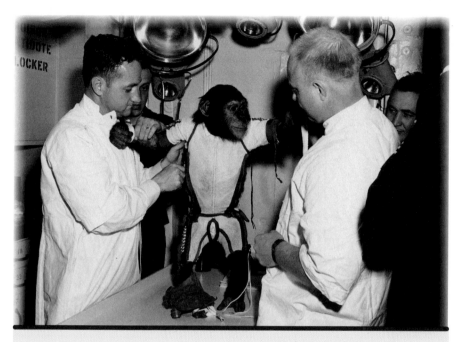

Ham receives a physical check by doctors. He was in great shape and ready for his mission.

received sips of water for quick, calm work. Always, there were hugs and playful moments with the trainers.[10]

For some chimps, the training was too hard. Being alone in small spaces was uncomfortable. Being strapped to man-made vehicles and feeling great speeds was unnatural. Enduring the motions of space travel was stressful. Born in the jungle, chimps were not used to the life of an astronaut. As they became upset or grew to be heavier than fifty pounds, they left the space school. Soon the group shrank to eighteen, and later to six, one of which would be the first chimp into space.

3

Blastoff

On January 2, 1961, the group of chimps traveled from New Mexico to Cape Canaveral, Florida. From there, the rocket, called a Mercury Redstone, would be launched. The trainers and chimps lived in a compound and worked in trailers. Ham became used to the new climate in Florida, which was wetter and more humid than the dry air of the New Mexico desert. Edward Dittmer carefully studied his behavior. He watched over Ham's nervous system, heart rate, breathing, and body temperature all the time. Daily, he placed electrodes, or wires, on Ham's body, which measured the activity of his heart. He secured plates to Ham's feet, which would mildly shock him if he was not concentrating on his work. He attached a band to Ham's body that sensed his lungs and monitored his respiration, or breathing.[1]

On January 30, 1961, six chimps took a final test. Ham hit his levers twenty-five times in twenty seconds, over and over again. He reacted in less than a second. He was the fastest and healthiest of all the chimps. His body and mind were strong, so he was the one chosen to go into space. "He was a well-tempered chimp," said Dittmer.[2]

If anything were to happen to Ham in the following

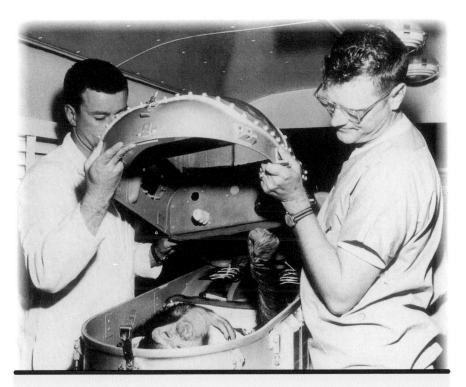

Edward Dittmer (right) closes the couch and checks for leaks. Ham will remain in the couch during his historic flight.

twenty-four hours, a forty-eight-pound female chimp would take his place. But at three years and seven months old, and thirty-seven pounds, Ham was ready for space.[3]

On the morning of January 31, 1961, Ham prepared for flight. He ate a breakfast of baby cereal, condensed milk, half an egg, cooking oil, gelatin, and vitamins. Dittmer dressed him in a web jacket, took him to the gantry, and placed him in the Mercury capsule. The capsule weighed about 2,000 pounds. It was a compartment shaped like a cone. It sat on top of a 66,000-pound Mercury Redstone rocket. Dittmer was a little anxious. He had seen other missiles go off track and explode over the ocean. He considered Ham quite a chimp, and wanted to see him live.[4] Dittmer strapped his freckled friend to a couch to protect him from the intense stress of takeoff and landing. As he had done so many times before, he wired the chimp with instruments that recorded heartbeat, breathing, and temperature. After he closed the lid on the capsule, Ham was alone, strapped inside a plastic chamber the size of a small trunk.

The chamber in which he sat, on a couch, was sealed off from the rest of the capsule. It had a supply of oxygen, which Ham would breathe. He would need it because in space there is no oxygen. In front of Ham, attached to the lid of the capsule, was an instrument panel with familiar lights and levers. He knew he had to

Ham looks out from inside the pressurized couch. The couch was loaded into the Mercury capsule on top of the rocket.

hit the lever and turn out the light. If he could hit the lever every twenty seconds and turn out the light every five, he would not feel a shock. Someone had placed a note in front of him, which only humans could understand. It read: "Have missile, will travel." It was the message of a carefree traveler, someone who would take a trip on a moment's notice. Although Ham's trip had been well planned, the people who had helped him reach this point needed to laugh a bit before letting him go. Ham bared his teeth as he took his position for flight. He was not smiling, but showing fear.[5]

Indeed, there were many things to fear. Five-foot waves crashed off the coast of Florida. The weather was grim. Ham was delayed over four hours in his capsule before he was launched. The 8:00 A.M. takeoff time came and went. The people responsible for Ham's flight did not want to rush. Christopher Kraft, the director of the flight, delayed the launch as he made decisions. He worried that Ham would not be able to wait, but other officers assured him that Ham could.[6] There were many problems to solve that morning, and Ham waited.

Inside the capsule, Ham was comfortably warm in a

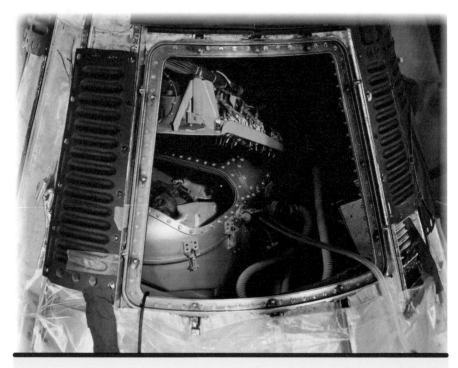

Ham's pressurized couch is inserted into the Mercury capsule.

space suit that felt to him about 65 °F (18 °C). However, the temperature elsewhere in the spacecraft was three times hotter. Ham had to wait until it cooled down. But after the power was turned on, the temperature rose again. Ham had to wait as the rocket cooled. The people checking the instruments that controlled Ham's environment were careful, but slow. Those who cleared things away from the launchpad took a long time. As those on the gantry tried to leave the area near the capsule, their elevator became stuck. Ham had to wait.

Then a small coil broke. As it was replaced, Ham waited for two more hours. He had waited since five-thirty that morning. Finally, at quarter to twelve, the lights in front of him began to shine. He started pulling levers. His mind and hands were active. Ten minutes later, he was launched.[7] Fire spewed from the tail of the rocket. Ham was on his way into space.

4

Accidents in Space

Blasting off, the rocket caused enormous vibrations. The rocket fuel burned, and gases spewed from the tail, pushing the thirty-three-ton missile toward the sky. Ham's whole body jiggled violently. He was pressed against his couch with extreme force. His lips curled back to reveal clenched teeth, which the flight engineers could see on a monitor. His heart pounded more quickly than usual. His breathing was rapid.[1] Every part of his body was alerted for danger. Gradually, the sensation passed.

Inside the chamber, Ham went to work. A white light flashed. Ham's slim fingers flattened the metal lever. There was time to spare. Pellets rolled noisily into a curved metal cup. Ham collected the food. His large lips seemed to kiss the prize as it was lowered to his teeth.

His eyes dashed back to the control panel. He ground the pellets with strong teeth, gnashing the beloved taste of banana. Blue light flashed; boom! Ham slapped the lever with a fast left hand. Pellets rolled like coins from a vending machine. Ham washed them down with a sip of water from a small tube.

Inside his chamber, everything worked well. Air pressed against his body in just the right way. On Earth, bodies press out and the air presses in. In space, there is no air. As a result, bodies press out too much in space. The air pressure inside Ham's capsule was carefully balanced to press on his body as it would on Earth. Oxygen flowed around him from a tank outside his chamber. Like a well-trained soldier, he slammed the levers flat. Absorbed by his work, he did not know that dangers were developing.[2]

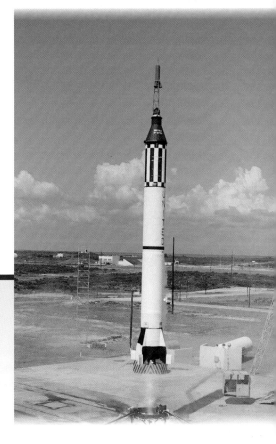

The Redstone rocket was used to launch Ham into flight. The black Mercury capsule sits on the top of the rocket. The yellow cherry picker (bottom right) would be used to rescue an astronaut from the capsule, if necessary, during countdown.

As the Mercury Redstone rocket tore away from Earth, accidents happened. The valve that let oxygen flow into Ham's chamber jiggled loose. This accident weakened the air pressure in the cabin outside of Ham's chamber. Luckily for Ham, the air pressure in his chamber remained balanced. However, there was another problem that did affect Ham.

During liftoff, the throttle of the rocket jammed open. A throttle controls the flow of fuel on all engines, from lawn mowers to rockets. Liquid oxygen, or lox, was the fuel for a Mercury Redstone rocket. Without a throttle, the lox flowed too quickly into the engine of the rocket. The lox burned out too soon. Fuel was feeding the rocket all at once, and the rocket blasted off with more power than planned. It had 52,000 pounds more thrust than was expected. For one second during its launch, the rocket went 7,540 feet per second instead of 6,465 feet per second. One hundred thirty-seven seconds after the rocket took off, it was out of gas. The Mercury Redstone rocket, or MR-2, was traveling too high, too fast.

A computer in the spacecraft sensed that things were going wrong in the engine chamber. There was an odd change in pressure because the liquid oxygen was gone. As a result, retro-rockets were fired. They are not supposed to fire until the rocket comes back toward Earth, to slow its speed. Instead, they were fired as the rocket climbed into space. This added an extra eight hundred miles per hour to the speed of Ham's craft.[3] He was moving into the atmosphere at 5,857 miles per hour.

He felt it. For one second, on his way up, he felt seventeen times heavier than he usually felt on Earth. The weight made his skin stretch across his bones. His body pressed hard against his aluminum space couch. Ham bared his teeth in fear.[4] He could not move. Ham did not know it, but he was fighting against one of the strongest forces in the universe. He was fighting against gravity.

Earth and everything on it are attracted to each other. Since Earth is so much larger, Earth pulls more strongly on the objects than the objects pull on Earth. This pull is what keeps everything on Earth. Living things are used to the gentle tug of gravity on their bodies. On Earth the pull of gravity made Ham feel about thirty-seven pounds. Scientists call the tug of gravity on a body on

The suit that Ham wore during his flight was made of mesh material and zippered up both sides.

Earth 1 g. During blastoff, Ham did not feel 1 g. He felt 17 gs, as if he weighed 629 pounds. Stuck against the back of his space couch, Ham may have felt as if he were a passenger in a speeding race car.

He saw the white lights flash, but his arms felt like lead. Reach the lever! He could not. Dzzzeeet! A shock of electricity came through his feet and sapped his strength. His body froze. Twice more, his right hand missed the lever. Twice more, he suffered a mild shock. Ham trusted his left hand. It was faster than his right. White light flashed, boom! Bananas and water fell for Ham. The game continued. Ham regained his skill. Lips puckered, brown eyes fastened on the instrument panel, and lanky arms flying, Ham beat the machine from there on in.

As he worked, Ham's capsule separated from the rocket, moving thousands of feet away. At his highest point from Earth he had climbed 157 miles. This height was forty-two miles higher than the capsule was supposed to climb. The malfunction at blastoff had thrust him farther than expected. At a certain point, Ham became so far from Earth that it no longer had as strong a pull on the mass of his capsule. For seven minutes, Ham felt no weight at all. He floated. A peaceful expression passed over his face.[5]

When Ham's capsule reached its highest point, it began to come down. Ham yawned to clear his ears because the pressure of the air around him was rapidly changing. Soon, his capsule began to fall toward Earth. It

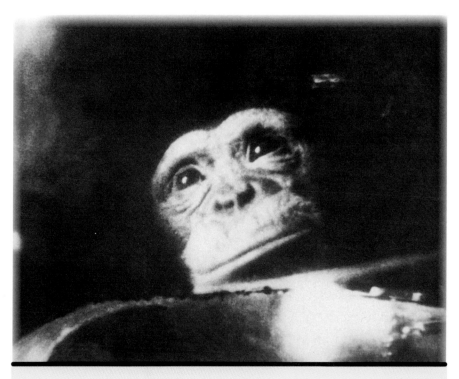

Ham was photographed during his flight by an automatic camera.

was gaining speed. It gathered more momentum than it was supposed to because it did not have the retro-rockets anymore. They were supposed to fire at this moment and slow him down. The speed crushed him into his couch again. Fifteen times the force he was used to on Earth pressed against his small body. That was only the beginning of his ride home.

He was about to feel the heat of reentry, when his capsule zipped from space to the air that living things breathe. In space, there is no air. Near Earth, the air wraps around the Earth like a blanket. It is called atmosphere. It is dense with gases that protect Earth from heat, cold, and dangerous rays of the Sun. The gases around Earth were like a wall for Ham's capsule to penetrate. His craft was going so fast that it pierced through the gases.[6] As the capsule reentered Earth's atmosphere, it disturbed the gases. They rubbed against Ham's craft. This rubbing is called friction.

The friction made Ham shake violently. His face hit the inside of the lid of his chamber, bruising his nose. He felt the pain, but could not touch his face with his arm because the force of reentry had pinned him to his couch. Everything bounced and bumped. Ham's whole body vibrated. His teeth clacked and the skin on his face wiggled. The lights before him blurred. A small yelp of pain just jiggled in his throat.

Outside, the friction caused tremendous heat. The capsule was as hot as flames. Fortunately, there was a saucer-shaped flap on it that protected Ham from the high temperature. It was called a heat shield. As planned, it kept Ham from feeling the intense heat of reentry. Close to the ocean, at ten thousand feet above Earth, the capsule's parachutes inflated. They ballooned out over his craft. Catching the air, they stopped the capsule from dropping too forcefully into the sea. These silent brakes slowed his capsule to a gentle landing. At this point, the heat shield was supposed to drop and anchor the capsule in the sea. It did not. The force of his fall into the ocean destroyed the heat shield. The heat shield disappeared.

This picture was taken by an automatic camera on board the Mercury spacecraft while Ham was inside.

There was nothing to steady the craft in the water. Ham's capsule began to flood. Water sloshed around the bottom of the capsule. Safe inside a chamber within the capsule, Ham was dry. He waited. In the Atlantic Ocean, the capsule bobbed like a cork. Eighteen inches of water flowed in. Ham kept dry and waited. Eight hundred pounds of water surrounded Ham. He waited. By then, Ham's furry face could have only peered out the plastic window of a capsule inside the capsizing ton of spacecraft. No one was rescuing him. Ham could only wait in his capsule alone.

5

Back on Earth

The recovery ships were in the wrong place. They were 290 miles downrange of the launching pad in Florida, ready to pick up the chimp. But Ham had traveled farther than that. His flight had been like a hastily lobbed wad of paper that misses the trash can. His trajectory, or path, had been higher and longer than people had planned. The farther and more forcefully a thing travels up, the farther and more forcefully it travels down. Ham was 420 miles out at sea, 130 miles farther than planned. His rocket had overshot its target. To correct that mistake, officers at Cape Canaveral sent Mayday messages, or pleas for help, to the naval officers who were waiting to rescue Ham.

They could not find him. For almost three hours, they

searched. Finally, a Navy plane spotted him. Two sailors from the ship USS *Ellison* quickly took a rubber raft to the crooked capsule and righted it. A helicopter arrived. Its blades whipped the water around Ham, making whitecaps. Eerily, dye escaped the wet capsule and turned the blue water green. Ham's craft was spent. The most important task at hand was to release him and take him home.

A marine lieutenant in the helicopter, George F. Cox, took control.[1] He used a long pole to guide a hook through a loop on Ham's bell-shaped capsule. The helicopter picked up the precious package and carried it to the recovery ship, the LSD *Donner*. The capsule was not going to sink, but the rescuers wondered: Was Ham alive?

The officers were quiet. What would they find when they opened the lid that Edward Dittmer had closed

A marine helicopter hoists the Mercury capsule, with chimpanzee Ham aboard, to a safe landing aboard the deck of the LSD Donner.

with such care and hope? All of a sudden, they heard a whimper. Major Benson, an Air Force veterinarian, opened the capsule.

"He's alive!" Benson cried.[2]

Ham bared his teeth. Every freckle on his face stood out. Patiently, he folded his arms and waited to be taken out of his couch. It had been an eight-hour ordeal. Only sixteen minutes of that time had been in flight. As politely as a guest arriving for dinner, Ham outstretched a soft palm to Benson. The two shook hands. Benson gave him an apple. Ham showed his teeth and took a bite.[3]

Ham was alive, but was he all right? Veterinarians rushed him to the battle-dressing station of the ship and gave him a thorough checkup. They found that he was tired and dehydrated. His body needed water.[4] The vets noticed a bruise on Ham's nose. Otherwise, he was fine. It was there and then that the chimp was given the name Ham. The letters of his name were short for Holloman Aeromedical, a laboratory that studied how people would react to zero gravity in space, and Hamilton Blackshear, the colonel in command of the space laboratory.

Newspaper and television reporters surrounded Ham. They flashed cameras and asked the Air Force officers if Ham would pose for photographs in his capsule. The chimpanzee's answer was no. He refused to return to the Mercury spacecraft.[5]

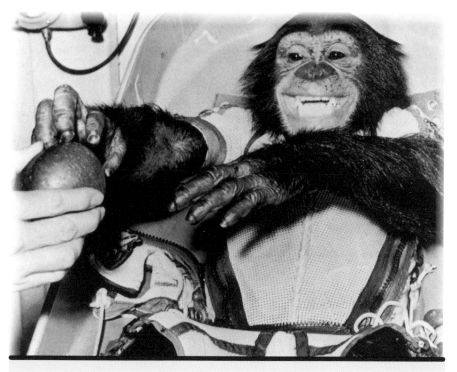

Ham reaches for an apple after a safe landing.

After his flight, Ham returned to the compound at Cape Canaveral, Florida. He ran into the arms of his beloved friend and trainer, Edward Dittmer. Dittmer was jubilant upon seeing Ham.[6] They played. Now there were many people who were proud of Ham. Everyone realized what Ham's flight meant. It had proved that an animal not only could survive spaceflight, but perform tasks there, too. Suddenly, Americans were confident that an astronaut could repeat Ham's success.

A man named Alan Shepard became the first American to do what Ham had done. Gus Grissom

A sailor carries Ham aboard the LSD Donner.

followed, and in 1961 Enos, another chimpanzee, orbited Earth three times. This successful flight helped make Earth orbit possible for American astronaut John Glenn. In the year 1969, three men went as far as the Moon. Neil Armstrong and Edwin "Buzz" Aldrin walked on the moon as Mike Collins watched from a spacecraft. People on Earth were thrilled. In their excitement about the future of space travel, many Americans forgot about Ham.

For the next seventeen years, Ham lived in a cage at the Washington National Zoo in the nation's capital. There, he lived alone, never making nests in trees, never grooming a friend. He ate. He slept. He stared at the children who came to the zoo. Sometimes he played by himself on the bars, hanging, swinging, but it was not like it was in his African home.

There, the jungles were dense and green and filled with other chimpanzees.

Ham and Edward Dittmer are happily reunited upon Ham's return to Cape Canaveral after his flight.

Even in the days just before his flight, there were other chimps around, training for possible missions in space. But at the Washington Zoo, Ham was all alone.

His keepers were kind. There were gorillas he could see in a cage nearby. But there were no chimpanzees for Ham to play with, and even his friend, Edward Dittmer, was gone, now working as a pilot in Vietnam.

Ham had been a hero. He had provided further evidence that human beings could survive in space and that America had the rockets to take them there. The humans who followed had gone all the way to the Moon. But Ham's reward for the role he had played was a life that had to be lonely and dull. Some people thought it was not very fair.

6

A Chance to Be Himself

Les Schobert was worried about Ham. Schobert was a director of a different kind of zoo, built in the hills of North Carolina. It was one of the first zoos in the world where the animals had lots of room. The chimps did not live in cages. They lived in a large tree-shaded space, many of them together. Schobert believed Ham would be happier there than he had been in a cage.[1]

At first, however, Ham was terrified. On September 24, 1980, he was loaded into a crate. It was a cold, rainy day. He bared his teeth at the strange new people who met him at the North Carolina Zoo. Soon he would learn that they were his friends, but at first they were frightening as they opened his crate and guided him into a temporary cage.

They watched him carefully, taking notes on everything he did. Ham could hear and smell the other chimps nearby, and after a while he was allowed to see and touch them through the bars.

Finally, after a month had gone by, the big moment came. Another chimp was brought to his cage. Her name was Maggie. She was a teenager, a little younger than Ham. For the first few minutes, he pretended not to like her. He roared and thrashed and beat his fists on the wall, and Maggie screamed and tried to get away. But the zookeepers knew it was only a show. Ham was big and strong by now, but he had lived for so many years by himself that he was not really sure how he ought to behave. He wanted the others to know he was tough.[2]

But Ham was also gentle and kind. He quickly accepted Maggie as his friend, and soon the two of them left the cage and joined the other chimps outside. It

Ham spent his later years at the North Carolina Zoological Park.

was a beautiful place. The sweet smell of flowers drifted down from the vines, and the chimps spent their days on a grassy hillside, playing in the cool shade of the trees.[3]

For Ham, it was not exactly like home. The African forests were still far away. But he was living now with other chimpanzees in a peaceful place, where most of them seemed to be happy and content.

Ham soon became the leader of the group. His hair was beginning to turn gray around his ears, a sign that he was now approaching middle age. He was twenty-four years old, and he moved a little slower than he did when he was young. But the other chimps liked him. When they became angry sometimes with each other, Ham would help them settle their disputes. He helped take care of the littlest chimp, a baby named Koby, and he and Maggie spent many hours together in the trees.

Nobody was sure how much Ham remembered. Did he think back about his flight into space? Did he remember his capsule bobbing in the sea, or the levers he had to push for banana pellets as his spacecraft soared past the gravity of Earth?

Whatever the answers, Les Schobert was happy that Ham, at last, was getting his reward. People did not ask much of him anymore. There were no trainers, and no experiments that he had to perform. There were only the children and their parents passing by and the company of the other chimpanzees.

"He is now getting a chance to live as a chimp," said Mr. Schobert. "We owe him that much."[4]

But then one winter day in 1983, Ham was not feeling well. He ate his afternoon meal at 3:30 P.M., then went and sat by himself in a corner.[5] A few minutes later, the zookeepers realized that he was dead. His friend Maggie was kneeling at his side, holding his hand, staring at the humans with her dark, steady eyes.

A sadness fell on the zoo after that. Ham had lived there for more than two years, and for a while at least he was the most famous chimpanzee in the country. When he died at the age of twenty-five, the victim apparently of a liver disease that none of his handlers knew that he had, people talked a lot about what he had done. "Ham the chimpanzee risked his life for his country," said *The Washington Post*, one of the most important newspapers in the nation.[6] He had helped pave the way for a journey to the Moon, and all of the human beings who knew him were impressed by his intelligence and gentle personality.

Those who cared for him at the zoo took comfort in the certain knowledge that Ham had been happy. They could feel his contentment every day beneath the trees. The humans who knew and understood him the best were glad about that. They were happy that Ham, the space hero, had finally gotten a chance to be himself.[7]

At the age of twenty-five, Ham died. But he had helped pave the way for America to safely enter space and land on the Moon.

GLOSSARY

air pressure—Pressure on an object caused by the weight of air.

astrochimp—A chimpanzee trained to survive spaceflight.

astronaut—A pilot or member of the crew of a spacecraft.

booster rocket—A rocket attached under the tail assembly of a missile or spacecraft to assist it in takeoff.

capsule—A compartment, shaped like a cone with its point lopped off, located atop a rocket.

chamber—An enclosed space or room inside a capsule.

electrode—A conductor through which an electrical current travels.

gantry—A bridgelike framework that spans over something for support, such as those used to build and service rockets.

heat shield—A shield located on the blunt end of a capsule. It is designed to absorb the heat and friction produced during the period of reentry as the capsule collides with more and more molecules of air in the atmosphere.

lox—Liquid oxygen, which is stored in one of two tanks inside a rocket.

missile—A self-propelled rocket, which can be launched from land, ships, or airplanes.

nervous system—The system of nerve fibers, nerve cells, and other nerve tissue in a person or animal by means of which impulses are received and interpreted.

orbit—The path of a man-made satellite about any heavenly body, or of one heavenly body around another.

retro-rockets—Backward-facing rockets mounted in the blunt end of a spacecraft that slow down the craft when fired.

rocket—A missile that, when fired, burns fuel. As the combustion gases thrust downward, the rocket is pushed up.

scaffold—A temporary raised framework for holding workers and materials.

test pilot—A pilot employed to test new or experimental aircraft by subjecting her or him to greater than normal stress.

web jacket—A nylon vest worn by chimps in training.

CHAPTER NOTES

Chapter 1. The Early Pioneers

1. Jane Goodall, "My Life Among Wild Chimpanzees," *National Geographic*, August 1963, pp. 282–287.

2. "Twenty-Fifth Anniversary of Ham the Astrochimp," *Spacelog*, vol. 3, no. 1, January 1986, p. 1.

3. Biographical Sketch, National Zoological Park, Smithsonian Institute, Washington, D.C., p. 1.

4. "Animals Go Into Space First," *Man in Space*, vol. 1, p. 52.

5. "Where Are They Now?" *Newsweek*, vol. 60, November 19, 1962, p. 26.

6. George M. House, "Project Mercury's First Passengers," *Spacelog*, vol. 8, no. 2, April–June 1991, p. 4.

7. "Animals Go Into Space First," p. 51.

8. House, p. 4.

Chapter 2. In the Lab

1. "Chimponauts in Training," *Time*, January 20, 1961, pp. 68–69.

2. George M. House, interview with Edward C. Dittmer, June 10, 1987 (Alamogordo: New Mexico State University at Alamogordo), transcript p. 11.

3. "From Jungles to the Lab: the Astrochimps," *Life*, vol. 50, February 10, 1961, p. 21.

4. "The Nearest Thing," *Time*, vol. 77, February 10, 1961, p. 58.

5. House, pp. 2, 4, 7, 10, 11.

6. Melinda Farbman, interview with Edward C. Dittmer, July 1999.

7. "From Jungles to the Lab: the Astrochimps," p. 21.

8. "Twenty-Fifth Anniversary of Ham the Astrochimp," *Spacelog*, vol. 3, no. 1, January 1986, p. 5.

9. "Chimps Readied for Three-Orbit Flight," *Missiles and Rockets*, November 13, 1961, p. 16.

10. House, p. 12.

Chapter 3. Blastoff

1. George M. House, interview with Edward C. Dittmer, June 10, 1987 (Alamogordo: New Mexico State University at Alamogordo), transcript p. 11.

2. Ibid.

3. "Mercury Flight Provides Severe Test for Capsule and Chimp," *Aviation Week*, vol. 74, February 6, 1961, pp. 26–28.

4. House, p. 12.

5. Frye Gaillard, "Ham the Space Chimp," *The Charlotte Observer*, July 26, 1981, p. 1B.

6. Loyd S. Swenson, Jr., James M. Grimwood, and Charles C. Alexander, *This New Ocean: A History of Project Mercury* (Washington, D.C.: NASA Historical Office, 1998), p. 314.

7. Ibid., p. 315.

Chapter 4. Accidents in Space

1. Kenneth F. Weaver, "School for Space Monkeys," *National Geographic*, vol. 119, no. 5, May 1961, pp. 729, 734.

2. "Animals Go Into Space First," *Man in Space*, vol. 1, p. 54.

3. M. Scott Carpenter et al., *We Seven* (New York: Simon & Schuster, 1962), p. 225.

4. Weaver, p. 729.

5. Ibid.

6. "Animals Go Into Space First," p. 55.

Chapter 5. Back on Earth

1. Kenneth F. Weaver, "School for Space Monkeys," *National Geographic*, vol. 119, no. 5, May 1961, p. 730.

2. "The Nearest Thing," *Time*, vol. 77, February 10, 1961, p. 59.

3. "U.S. Widens Its Lead in the Space Race," *U.S. News and World Report*, February 13, 1961, p. 46.

4. "Project Mercury's First Passengers," *Spacelog*, vol. 8, no. 2, April–June 1991, p. 5.

5. "Twenty-Fifth Anniversary of Ham the Astrochimp," *Spacelog*, vol. 3, no. 1, January 1986, p. 5.

6. George M. House, interview with Edward C. Dittmer, June 10, 1987 (Alamogordo: New Mexico State University at Alamogordo), transcript p. 12.

Chapter 6. A Chance to Be Himself

1. Frye Gaillard, "Ham the Space Chimp," *The Charlotte Observer*, July 26, 1981, p. 1B.

2. Ibid.

3. Ibid.

4. Frye Gaillard, interview with Les Schobert, July 1981.

5. "Ham, Retired Space Chimp, Dead at 25 1/2," *Science*, April 1983, p. 12.

6. "The Right Stuff," *The Washington Post*, January 21, 1983, p. A16.

7. Gaillard, "Ham the Space Chimp," p. 1B.

FURTHER READING

Books

Baird, Anne. *The U.S. Space Camp Book of Rockets.* New York: William Morrow and Co., Inc., 1994.

Marko, Katherine M. *Animals in Orbit: Monkeynauts and Other Pioneers in Space.* New York: Franklin Watts, 1991.

Snedden, Robert. *Rockets and Spacecraft.* Austin, Tex.: Raintree Steck-Vaughn Publishers, 1998.

Vogt, Gregory. *Apollo and the Moon Landing.* Brookfield, Conn.: The Millbrook Press, 1991.

Internet Addresses

Marshall, John. "Pets in Space." *Bad Air and Space Museum.* 1997. <http://badairandspace.com/petsinspace.htm> (January 26, 2000).

NASA. "Earth Science Enterprise." *For Kids Only.* July 15, 1999. <http://kids.earth.nasa.gov/> (January 26, 2000).

NASA. *Mercury 7 Archives.* March 29, 1999. <http://www.ksc.nasa.gov/history/mercury/mercury.html> (January 26, 2000).

NASA. *NASA Human Spaceflight.* <http://spaceflight.nasa.gov/index-n.html> (January 26, 2000).

INDEX